Coming Soon...

FLIES TASTE WITH THEIR FEET
WEIRD FACTS ABOUT INSECTS

BABOONS WAITED ON TABLES IN ANCIENT EGYPT!

WEIRD FACTS ABOUT ANCIENT CIVILIZATIONS

A WEIRD-BUT-TRUE BOOK

by
Melvin & Gilda Berger
Illustrated by Robert Roper

SCHOLASTIC INC.
New York Toronto London Auckland Sydney

Special thanks to Doric Wilson

ISBN 0-590-93779-0

12 11 10 9 8 7 6 5 4 3 2   7 8 9/9 0 1/0

Printed in the U.S.A.   40

First Scholastic printing, November 1996

ANCIENT EGYPT

(3100 B.C.–300 B.C.)

BABOONS WAITED ON TABLES IN ANCIENT EGYPT

The Egyptians trained baboons to serve food and clear tables. What's more, they taught these big monkeys to pick figs from trees for their masters. (If you have a fig tree, you could try this!)

DID YOU KNOW?

- Today certain monkeys help people who are paralyzed to eat, dress, and care for themselves. A restaurant in Holland has two chimpanzees that bring food and pour drinks.

LAUGH LINES

Why did the Egyptians use baboons?

They worked for peanuts!

HOLY CATS

The Eyptians believed cats were sacred — and kept many as pets. The government passed strict laws against hurting these adored animals. Anyone caught injuring a cat was put to death — even if the cat lived!

CAT ATTACK

The Persian King Cambyses II captured city after city in Egypt. Finally he reached Memphis. But his soldiers could not scale the high wall around the city.

The Egyptian love of cats gave Cambyses an idea. He had his soldiers round up hundreds of cats and throw them over the wall. The horrified Egyptians opened the gates and surrendered!

ACHING TEETH

The Egyptians got toothaches from eating bread! Desert sand blew into the growing grain, mixed with the flour, and became part of the baked bread. Eating bread in ancient Egypt was like munching on sandpaper. It was enough to set one's teeth on edge!

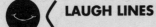

LAUGH LINES

An Egyptian Riddle
What goes on four legs in the morning, two legs at noon, and three legs at night?

Humans! We crawl on all fours as babies, walk on two legs most of our lives, and use a cane when very old!

HATCHING EGGS

The Egyptians hatched chicken eggs in a bizarre way. They buried the eggs in hills of dung! The dung warmed the eggs — and they hatched as though warmed by hens.

A PIG'S EYE

Egyptian doctors treated blindness with the eye of a pig! To the pig's eye, they added honey and red dye. Then they mashed everything together and poured it into the blind person's *ear*! No one knows if the cure helped anyone to see. But it sure left a lot of pigs with only one eye!

BLOODSUCKERS

Doctors believed many diseases were caused by "bad" blood. So they put 1-inch worms, called leeches, on sick people. The leeches bit through the skin and *sucked* out blood. The patients said this made them feel better. Were they cured — or were they just happy to be rid of the bloodsuckers?

DID YOU KNOW?

- **Today some doctors still use leeches after skin surgery. The worms help reduce the pain and swelling.**

ROCK-A-BYE

Egyptians used to sleep with stone headrests. No wonder so many woke up in the morning with headaches!

OUCH!

Rich Egyptian women often pulled out all the hairs on their heads — including eyebrows and eyelashes! Then they rubbed the tops of their heads with a cloth to make them shiny. What some people will do to look beautiful!

DID YOU KNOW?

- Both sexes wore makeup. Women with eyebrows painted them gray, black, or green.

CAUGHT RED-HANDED

Like some women today, Egyptian women painted their fingernails red. But they didn't stop there. They also smeared red paint on the palms of their hands and the soles of their feet!

GREASE CONES

Trendy Egyptian women wore large cones of perfumed wax on top of their wigs. As the day went on, the wax melted. The drippings made their faces shiny — and the perfume made them smell good.

SCHOOL DAYS

Priests ran the schools in Egypt. They punished the students without mercy.

DID YOU KNOW?

- The few boys who went to school learned to read and write hieroglyphs—a picture language.

BURIAL FOR A CAT

Wealthy families mummified their dead cats. They placed the cat mummy inside a coffin and set it in a tomb. The owner also placed mice mummies inside the tomb — to feed the kitty in its afterlife!

DID YOU KNOW?

- Egyptians showed their sorrow at the death of a pet cat by shaving off their eyebrows.

A MUMMY IS NOT A MOMMY

Egyptians believed in life after death. So they prepared the dead for the afterlife by turning them into mummies! (Warning! Do not try this at home!)

Workers first removed the corpse's heart, lungs, and stomach. Then they poked a long iron hook through the nose to pull out the brain!

Next they packed a special kind of salt inside and around the body. They left it there for 2 months. The salt dried out all of the body's blood and water.

Afterwards they soaked the body in wine and rubbed it with spices. Finally, they covered the figure with jewels and wrapped it in a 3-mile-long strip of linen bandage!

DID YOU KNOW?

- **Some mummies are covered with up to twenty layers of linen wrapping.**

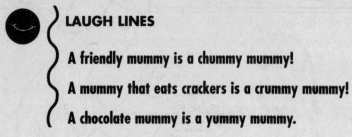

A friendly mummy is a chummy mummy!

A mummy that eats crackers is a crummy mummy!

A chocolate mummy is a yummy mummy.

SERVANTS FOREVER

Early kings in Egypt had statues of their servants buried with them. They believed these figures would serve them in the afterlife.

Later kings felt this was not good enough. They had their servants killed and put into their tombs! The worst was King Zer. He had 338 servants sacrificed at his funeral!

DID YOU KNOW?

- Pyramids contained everything the king would need in the afterlife—including a toilet.

READY AND SET

The rich dead were laid out flat with arms crossed on their chests. They were made to look as if they were asleep and would soon awaken.

But servants or slaves were buried in a stooping position. They had to appear ready to spring up and serve their masters.

MUDDY MOURNERS

When a man died, the women in his family mourned in public. They smeared their faces with mud and wandered the streets screaming and beating themselves on their chests.

THE WAY TO GO

Tutankhamen's four-room tomb held more than five thousand beautiful objects. Many were covered with gold. His coffin itself was made of gold. And a magnificent painted gold mask covered the mummy's head and shoulders. Talk about being worth your weight in gold!

DID YOU KNOW?

- Tutankhamen's tomb is the only ancient tomb to be found almost complete. For centuries the entrance was blocked by rocks thrown there by workers digging another royal tomb.

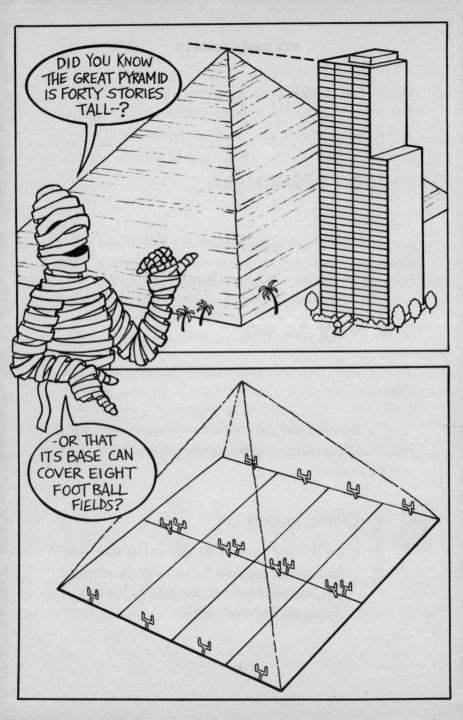

OUT OF SIGHT

The magnificent Great Pyramid was built around 2600 B.C. as a tomb for the king, or pharaoh, Khufu. But it seems that King Khufu was never placed inside! No one knows why.

DID YOU KNOW?

- **The Great Pyramid at Giza is as tall as a 40-story skyscraper. It was the tallest building in the world until the Eiffel Tower was built in 1889. Eight football fields could fit on the 13-acre base of the pyramid!**

LAUGH LINES

As one mummy said to another, "I don't mind being buried in a pyramid. But the view is awful!"

A BIG JOB

The workers on the Great Pyramid dug up, cut, moved, and set in place over two million giant blocks of stone! The average block weighed as much as two cars (2 1/2 tons). Because the wheel had not yet been invented, the Egyptians probably dragged the stones on heavy sleds called sledges.

Most of the builders were farmers, not slaves. Every summer the Nile River flooded. The farmers could not till the soil. So the government put them to work on the pyramids. How were they paid? Mostly with garlic and radishes!

DID YOU KNOW?

- It took about 100,000 men some 20 years to build the Great Pyramid.

LAUGH LINES

Did you hear about the mummy who said, "I wouldn't be caught dead in a pyramid!"?

STRING ALONG

The pyramid builders didn't have rulers or yardsticks. Instead they measured with pieces of knotted string. Yet, their measurements could not be beat. The Great Pyramid has only a single mistake. One side is off by a half inch!

PHARAOH'S FIB

Pharaoh Ramses II lost the Battle of Kadesh around 1285 B.C. But in those days there was no TV to report the news. When Ramses returned home, he told everyone that he had won! He even put up a monument to his victory. It took years for people to learn the truth.

A QUEEN WITH A BEARD

The queen of Egypt, Cleopatra, thought of herself as king. In court she dressed in mens' clothing and wore a fake beard. She insisted that people speak of her as "*His* Majesty!"

 LAUGH LINES

JOE: What Egyptian queen liked spaghetti?
MOE: Cleopasta!

DEAD AWAKENING

King Ramses I died around 1290 B.C. About 3,000 years later, workers opened his tomb. They took out the mummy and placed it on the ground. The hot sun melted the resin in the linen bandage. Horror-struck, everyone saw the arm of the long-dead king lift and wave! King or not, no one waved back!

DID YOU KNOW?

- People who dug up mummies sometimes chopped them into pieces. Sick people ate the body parts, thinking they would cure their diseases.

LAUGH LINES

DAN: Why was the mummy so jumpy?

NAN: Because it was all wound up!

TALES FROM THE TOMB

Workers found one mummy with blood clotted in his hair and a gaping wound in his skull. His face was twisted in agony. Someone must have been in a big hurry to mummify him!

ANCIENT GREECE

(2000 B.C.–200 B.C.)

WALKING THROUGH WALLS

Many houses in ancient Greece were made of mud bricks. The bricks were not very hard. Burglars didn't break into a house through a door or window. They just dug their way in through a wall!

SOUP OR SLOP

Among the Greeks, the bravest and most daring were the Spartans. They ate a black soup made of pieces of pork, pig blood, salt, and vinegar that most people agreed tasted horrible. But it was supposed to be very healthy. After tasting the soup a visitor said, "Now I know why Spartans are not afraid to die!"

DID YOU KNOW?

- A Spartan had to be married by age 30 or he was not allowed to vote.

A TASTE FOR RELIGION

The ancient Greeks sometimes ate the flesh of priests at religious ceremonies. Eating priests' flesh, the Greeks thought, made them holy.

DID YOU KNOW?

- **Through the centuries, flesh-eating has been part of some religions.**

SET SAIL

Every Greek corpse was buried with a coin in its mouth. The money was to pay the boatman, Charon. In Greek legend, Charon sailed the ferry that carried the dead to the underworld.

DID YOU KNOW?

- **Poor people in Greece often carried money in their mouths instead of in purses.**

FAMILY STYLE

The ancient Greeks had an unusual way of honoring a dead family member. They ate parts of the corpse! This was to show respect and to keep the dead person's soul within the family.

LAUGH LINES

Why did the man refuse to eat his dead uncle?

Because he was fed up with people!

BOTTOMS UP

Queen Artemisia built a giant tomb to hold the ashes of her dead husband King Mausolus. The splendid structure is one of the seven wonders of the ancient world. This led to the word *mausoleum*, which means a large tomb.

Finally the time came to put Mausolus's ashes in the tomb. But Artemisia refused to part with her husband's remains. Instead, she poured his ashes into her wine and drank them!

STARK NAKED

Orsippus was a slow runner. No one expected him to win a race at the Olympics of 720 B.C. But while running, his loincloth fell off! He ran the rest of the race completely bare. And he came in first!

Other Greek male athletes thought this a great idea. From then on, they all competed in the nude!

DID YOU KNOW?

- Only men took part in the Olympics. But women had their own races at the Games of Hera.

LAUGH LINES

A GREEK RIDDLE
If we catch it, we throw it away. If we can't catch it we keep it. What is it?

A flea!

BLOODY SPORT

Ancient Greek boxers fought while seated. They wrapped their hands and arms with leather thongs.

Sharp metal spikes stuck out on all sides. Helpers strapped the fighters into heavy stone chairs facing each other. At a signal, the boxers started punching and kicking each other until one was killed!

DID YOU KNOW?

- **The champion Greek boxer was Theogenes. He killed nearly 1,500 opponents.**

SKY BOMB

An eagle carrying a turtle in its beak flew over the playwright Aeschylus. The giant bird seemed to be looking for a rock on which to crack the turtle's shell. Thinking Aeschylus's bald head was a rock, the bird dropped the turtle. You can probably guess what happened next. Poor Aeschylus!

DID YOU KNOW?

- **Some years before, a fortune-teller told Aeschylus he would die by a blow from the heavens.**

LAUGH LINES

Why was Aeschylus surprised when the turtle fell on him?

Nothing like that had entered his head before!

THE AMAZING MILO

At one Olympics, Milo of Crotona walked around the entire stadium carrying a 4-year-old cow on his back. Then, with one blow of his fist, he killed the animal! The cow was cooked and Milo ate all the meat! This was quite a change from his usual daily diet of 20 loaves of bread washed down with 18 pints of wine!

Milo once attended a feast at the home of his wife's father. Suddenly the roof began to shake and break apart. The mighty Milo held up the ceiling while the guests fled! As soon as everyone was safely away, Milo ducked out. Seconds later, the whole roof caved in.

Milo often walked alone in the woods. One day he came upon a huge log that was partly split. Milo tried to pull the wood apart with his bare hands. But the log sprang closed, trapping his hands inside. Wild animals attacked the helpless man. Within a few days, the powerful athlete was dead.

THE AMAZING MILO

LATER...

BRIGHT IDEA

Archimedes, the Greek inventor, lived in the city of Syracuse. When the Roman navy attacked, Archimedes was asked to help defend his hometown. The inventor collected some huge mirrors and focused the sun's hot rays on the Roman ships. Hooray for Archimedes. Within minutes, the ships caught fire and sank!

WHAT WILL THE NEIGHBORS SAY?

Archimedes was taking a bath. He noticed that water slopped over the top as he lowered his body into the tub. Suddenly he understood the basic idea of buoyancy.

Very excited, Archimedes dashed out naked into the street. "Eureka! Eureka!" he shouted. He had learned about buoyancy — but he forgot his clothes!

DID YOU KNOW?

- *Eureka* means "I have found it" in Greek. We still say "Eureka" when we're excited.

DR. ELEPHANT

King Porus of India battled the Greeks while seated on an elephant. Several Greek arrows struck Porus and he fell to the ground badly wounded. One version of the tale says that the elephant pulled out all the arrows with his trunk!

SHAVE AND A HAIRCUT

Alexander the Great was the outstanding general of the ancient world. Before going into battle he had his soldiers shave all the hair off their heads and faces. His reason? To stop enemies from grabbing the men by the hair to cut off their heads!

SWEET HEREAFTER

Alexander the Great died at the age of 32. His followers buried him in a glass coffin filled with honey. How sweet!

DID YOU KNOW?

- Ancient people knew that honey never spoils. Honey that is thousands of years old still tastes good.

ANCIENT ROME

(750 B.C.—A.D. 470)

PIGGING OUT

Rich Romans often ate too much at holiday feasts. Yet even when they were full they didn't want to stop eating. So what did they do? They built a special room next to the dining room. They called it the *vomitorium*. You can probably guess what that was for!

DID YOU KNOW?

- There were so many Roman holidays that the emperor set a limit—135 holidays a year. That's about one every three days!

FREAKY FEASTS

Like other wealthy Romans, Emperor Heligabalus (A.D. 204–222) served his guests expensive and unusual foods. In fact, the more way-out the better.

At one dinner party, the slaves brought out six hundred ostrich brains! Another menu included peas with gold pieces, rice with pearls, and lentils with jewels! Can you imagine "richer" foods?

Emperor Heligabalus also had a gross sense of humor. One time he collected some animal bladders. He had the slaves blow them up like balloons and stick them under the cushions of his guests' couches. When the guests sat down, the bladders burst with a very embarrassing *pfffft-plop*!

DID YOU KNOW?

• Guests ate lying down on couches. They leaned on one elbow while picking at the food with their fingers.

A BERRY NICE BATH

Wealthy Roman women bathed at home — in berry juice! They mixed together 20 pounds of crushed strawberries and 2 pounds of crushed raspberries. The berries might not have gotten them very clean. But they sure gave the skin a healthy red glow!

? | **DID YOU KNOW?**

- Most people bathed in public bathhouses. Slaves rubbed the bathers with olive oil (soap hadn't been invented) and scraped them clean with curved metal tools called *strigils*.

IN COLD BLOOD

The Romans believed that the dead needed blood for their life after death. The blood came from slaves or prisoners who were forced to fight to the death at the funeral.

? | **DID YOU KNOW?**

- The funeral fights were also thought to honor the dead person and to help cheer up the mourners.

MAN AGAINST MAN

The funeral fights grew into public entertainments. The fighters, called gladiators, appeared before huge crowds. Some wore armor and carried a sword and a shield. Others had nets and snagged opponents before spearing them.

DID YOU KNOW?

- Champion gladiators became as famous as today's film stars.

MAN AGAINST ANIMAL

The Romans often forced gladiators to fight wild bears, elephants, lions, or tigers. They also let starving beasts attack condemned criminals or Christians. Sometimes they had only a knife for protection. More often they had no weapon at all.

TOUGH LAWS

In fifth century Rome the laws were very strict. A citizen could be put to death for:
- "singing insulting songs" about a high official!
- cheating a customer!
- "making disturbances in the city at night!"
- publishing lies!

DID YOU KNOW?

- Julius Caesar issued the very first traffic law. It banned all vehicles with wheels from the city of Rome from sunrise to sunset.

LOVE NOTES

The Romans jailed St. Valentine, an early Christian, for refusing to worship their gods. But the good man was known to love children. Many boys and girls tossed love notes into his jail cell. Perhaps that's why we now celebrate Valentine's Day with cards to people we love.

LAUGH LINES

One Valentine's Day I got a note that said, "I'd like to spend more time with you after school." Unfortunately it was from my teacher!

FATHER POWER

In ancient Rome the father ruled the roost. He had total control over all members of the family. If he wished, he could sell his children into slavery or have them killed. As long as he lived, the father was boss — even over married children and their sons and daughters!

DID YOU KNOW?

- Parents chose marriage partners for their children. Most boys married around age 16, girls when they were 14.

NEW HEADS FOR OLD

Rulers came and went in ancient Rome. So the sculptors put removable heads on statues of famous people. Then, when someone was murdered and someone else came to power, the sculptor merely put on a new head!

DID YOU KNOW?

- Roman wives who wanted to kill their husbands often used the poison found on the skin of certain toads.

A REAL NIGHTMARE

In a dream, Julius Caesar's wife saw a statue of her husband with blood running out of it. She awoke frightened and begged Caesar to stay home. But he went out. Later that day his friend Brutus and some twenty other men stabbed Caesar to death!

DID YOU KNOW?

• **Caesar was killed because he was taking over the government and becoming a dictator.**

LAUGH LINES

How did the Roman cut his hair?

He used a pair of Caesars (scissors)!

SHOW OF SHOWS

Emperor Julius Caesar once staged a very bizarre show. He had five hundred foot soldiers, sixty soldiers on horseback, and twenty elephants fight for his entertainment! Not to be outdone, another emperor flooded a stadium and held a naval battle. The public had the added "fun" of watching people drown.

DEATH TRAP

Slaves sometimes drove chariots in Circus Maximus, the biggest arena in Rome. The prize for winning was freedom. But there was a catch. The long, oval arena had sharp, dangerous curves at either end. That's where many of the speeding chariots toppled and crashed. Few drivers ever lived to be free men.

DID YOU KNOW?

- **Romans only used chariots for races and parades, never for war.**

LAUGH LINES

HARRY: **This chariot is called Lightning.**

LARRY: **Is it very fast?**

HARRY: **No, but it strikes trees!**

BAD GUY

The Emperor Nero was not much of a family man. When young, he had his mother murdered. Three years later he divorced his wife and killed her. After that he murdered his second wife.

Nero later wanted to poison his half brother, Brittanicus. But Brittanicus had a food taster who tried part of each dish or drink to make sure it was safe. Yet the evil Nero was able to outsmart his half brother.

Nero served Brittanicus some warm wine. The taster found it all right. But Brittanicus thought it too hot. So he added cold water. After a few sips he fell down dead. How come? Nero had added poison to the water, not the wine!

Some say Nero fiddled while Rome burned. But this cannot be. There were no fiddles, or violins, in ancient Rome. But Nero may have started Rome's terrible fire in the year A.D. 64. It is said that he wanted people to see the flames behind him as he recited a poem on the burning of Troy!

HORSING AROUND

Emperor Caligula loved his horse more than you can believe. He appointed it ruler, or consul, of Rome! He built the horse a stable of ivory and invited it to eat at his table. The horse even drank wine from its own golden cup!

LAUGH LINES

What did Caligula's horse say when it finished dinner?

"That's the last straw!"

FLY CEMETERY

The poet Virgil once killed a fly. But he didn't just toss it away. Virgil held a fancy funeral and buried the insect in a tomb near the poet's home!

This was not as crazy as it seems. The Romans taxed houses, but not cemeteries. The fly tomb made the land around Virgil's house a cemetery. So he did not have to pay any taxes!

SLOW SAILING

Roman General Mark Antony lost an important naval battle in the year 31 B.C. The reason? His sailors could hardly pull their oars through the water!

Later the sailors found out what had happened. Hundreds of sucker fish had attached themselves to the oars. The weight of the fish made it almost impossible to row!

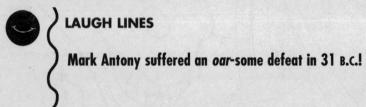

LAUGH LINES

Mark Antony suffered an *oar*-some defeat in 31 B.C.!

HEAD MAN

The Roman General Marcus Crassus lost a major battle with the Parthians. Afterwards, the Parthian general invited Crassus to dine with him. The outcome was ghastly. Instead of getting dinner, Crassus got his head cut off! The Parthians then filled the mouth with melted gold and shipped the head back home — where it was used as a prop in stage plays!

DID YOU KNOW?

- **Crassus was famous for having crushed the slave revolt led by the gladiator Spartacus.**

A PICK A NUMBER

The Romans had a special way of writing their numbers.

> One was I.
> Five was V.
> Ten was X.

Experts think the Roman numerals may have been based on the hand. *I* looks like 1 finger sticking up. *V* looks like all 5 fingers pressed together. And *X* looks like 2 hands crossed.

OOPS!

Ptolemy, a Roman astronomer, drew maps that Christoper Columbus used on his voyage one thousand years later. The maps showed Spain and China close together. They gave Columbus the courage to set sail to China. He soon learned that the maps were wrong. But thanks to Ptolemy, Columbus discovered America!

OTHER ANCIENT
CIVILIZATIONS

ANCIENT MESOPOTAMIA
(3500 B.C. – 540 B.C.)

A STEP UP

The citizens of ancient Mesopotamia used to dump their garbage in the streets. Soil blew over the garbage and people tramped on it. The street level grew higher and higher. Soon the streets were higher than the floors of the houses. There was only one thing to do — raise the floors!

DID YOU KNOW?

- The Mesopotamians made the floors higher by adding a thick layer of clay.

ANCIENT BABYLON
(1750 B.C. – 538 B.C.)

SHADY DOINGS

The first umbrellas date back to ancient Babylon. At first only kings and nobles used umbrellas. They used them to keep off the sun's rays — not the rain! Later, ordinary people had umbrellas.

DID YOU KNOW?

• The ancient Romans were the first to use umbrellas in the rain. By the 1700s, people all over Europe were carrying umbrellas on rainy days.

EVERYONE'S A DOCTOR

Babylonians had a weird way of treating the sick. The families put the patient on a bed out in the street! According to the law, anybody who knew about the illness had to stop and offer advice!

LAUGH LINES

FATHER OF THE PATIENT: My son has trouble breathing.

PASSER-BY: I know a medicine to stop that!

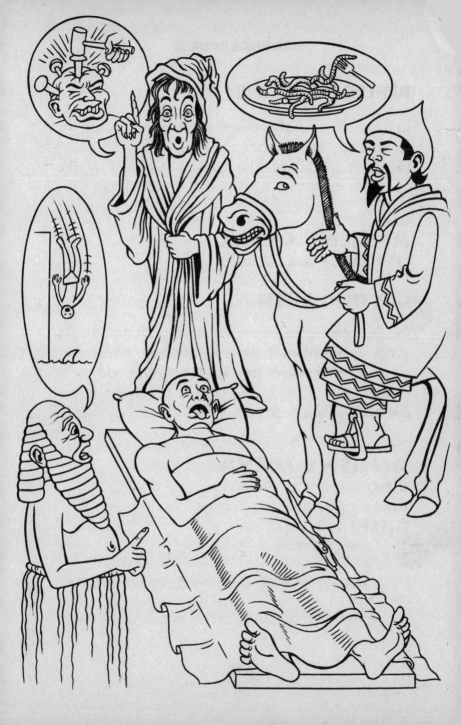

BITTER MEDICINE

In Babylon, if a patient died while being treated for an infection, the doctor had his hands cut off! If the victim was a slave, the doctors had to buy the owners a new slave.

ANCIENT CHINA
(1770 B.C. - A.D. 1280)

GETTING EVEN

Insults were dangerous in ancient China. To get even, the insulted person would buy some tiger whiskers, chop them into small bits, and add them to the enemy's food. Once inside the stomach, the tasteless whiskers cause terrible pain and sickness.

ANCIENT MAYAS
(600 B.C. - A.D. 900)

OUCH!

The ancient Mayas filed their teeth to a point for the sake of beauty. Then they drilled a hole in each tooth and put in a colorful jewel! Maybe their teeth looked pretty. But what a pain to get them that way!

DON'T DRINK THE WATER

Mayan priests sacrificed young girls to Chac, the rain god. They covered the girls with jade and silver jewelry. Then they marched them to the edge of a 60-foot-deep well and threw them in. The weight of the jewels kept them from escaping.

BASEMENT BURIALS

Mayas painted their corpses red. They then wrapped the dead in straw mats along with some personal belongings. The bodies were buried in graves dug under the floor of the houses in which they had lived. What a short trip to the underworld!

VIKINGS
(A.D. 800 – A.D. 1100)

LAUNCH TIME

The Vikings used to sacrifice humans on the prow of new boats before placing the boats in the water. They believed the human spirits would protect the ship. The modern custom of breaking a bottle of

champagne over the prow of a new ship comes from
the old Viking blood sacrifices.

LAUGH LINES

I won't say the boat wasn't well-built. But when
the lady hit the prow with the champagne bottle—
the prow broke!

LIVING TERRORS

Viking warriors used to eat mushrooms that
contained certain chemicals. These chemicals drove
the Vikings crazy. In their madness they killed, stole,
and burned without mercy. The worst of the Vikings
were called *berserkers*.

DID YOU KNOW?

• The word berserk still describes a person who acts
  wildly.

THE BIG LIE

About A.D. 982 the Viking Erik the Red discovered
an island in the North Atlantic Ocean. It looked

white because it was covered by snow all year long. But he wanted people to settle there. So he named the island *Green*land!

DID YOU KNOW?

- **Erik the Red's son, Leif, was probably the first European to land on North America.**

ANCIENT INCA
(A.D. 1100–A.D. 1532)

HOLES IN THE HEAD

Inca warriors cut holes in the skulls of enemies they killed in battle. The soldiers wore a piece of the bone as a good luck charm. Lucky for them — but not for their enemies!

DID YOU KNOW?

- **Many Inca skulls have been found with small holes in them. Experts think that doctors cut out pieces of skulls to treat headaches, mental disease, and head injuries.**

SURPRISE ATTACK

Inca Emperor Atahualpa went to the baths on the day of his coronation in 1532. On the way out he was captured by the invading Spaniards. Without their leader, the powerful Inca army was soon defeated by the small group of Spaniards. The vast Inca empire was lost because of a bath!

DID YOU KNOW?

- **The Incas offered the Spaniards a room filled with gold as ransom for Atahualpa. But the Spaniards killed him before the gold arrived. To this day, no one has found the gold offered to the Spaniards.**

ANCIENT AZTECS
(A.D. 1325 – A.D. 1521)

BLOND IDOL

The Spanish explorer, Hernando Cortés, had only one hundred men and a few cannons when he tried to conquer the mighty Aztecs. He didn't get far until, suddenly, the Aztec soldiers flung down their arms and dropped to their knees!

Cortés soon discovered the reason for the weird behavior. The Aztecs had spotted a Spanish officer with blond hair and a long beard. They had never seen anyone like this before. He had to be a god! After that, Cortés had no trouble with his conquest.

SPICY CHOCOLATE

The Aztecs were among the first people to make and eat chocolate. But they ate it in a strange way. They added hot, mouth-burning peppers!

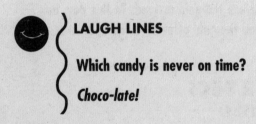

LAUGH LINES

Which candy is never on time?

Choco-late!